Gianni Bereng

MW00625341

# Italians
# Italiener

Edited by / Herausgegeben von
Susanna Berengo Gardin

For this edition:
© 2000 te Neues Verlag GmbH, Kempen
For the original edition:
© 1999 Federico Motta Editore S.p.A., Milan
All rights reserved.
For the photographs:
© 1999 Gianni Berengo Gardin, in Italy represented by Agenzia Contrasto-Roma

The photographs in this book have not been altered in any way, nor „improved"
by any form of computer technique.

Original book title: Italiani. Gianni Berengo Gardin

English translation: Anthony Vivis
German translation: Yvette Wiesenthal
Production: SWB Communications, Dr. Sabine Werner-Birkenbach, Marbach

Die Deutsche Bibliothek – CIP-Einheitsaufnahme
Ein Titeldatensatz für diese Publikation ist bei der Deutschen Bibliothek erhältlich

ISBN 3-8238-5453-4
Printed in Italy

# Contents / Inhalt

## One Country – Many Lands

„Photography has to face one main challenge which other media can conceal or at least veil much more easily or cynically. The challenge is to make something fundamentally paradoxical both visible and disturbingly realistic in an art form that veers between supreme artifice and ultimate objectivity. Like alchemy, photography is expected to show us all the parts that make up the whole. It is as if fundamentals – like feeling, instinct, and gestures – cannot be recognised in other forms of art or communication, as they are too adulterated, run-down, impure. Photography, however, is expected to capture the purity of a fleeting moment, to conserve it geologically, as a chink in rock or a fossil. In other words, photos must preserve for posterity things that would otherwise rapidly disappear, apparently unnoticed, in the turbulent torrent of events – either real or imaginary."

I wrote this a few years ago in the Introduction to an exhibition of work by young photographers. Since that time the „videocentricity" of Italian culture has grown even more sterile, which indicates how relieved I was to step inside the world of Berengo Gardin. It reinforces my own view that whereas we think of television as „up-to-the-minute" and photography as „old-fashioned", the truth is often the reverse. Television is conservative, woolly, and generally avoids anything complex. Photography, on the other hand, is inquisitive – it opens things up and tracks things down. Here, I am not talking about the deadly repetitiveness of fashion-photos or of pseudo-innovative advertising pictures, which inter-relate – symbiotically and not by accident – with television. I am referring to the kind of photography that produces pictures which still have the power to „take us by surprise".

Any book of photos – by a professional or not – strikes me as being a lot more varied than a televisual palimpsest. Whenever we switch the TV on we see the same faces on every channel. This amounts to a kind of morbid atavistic ritual, an unhappy form of self-fertilisation. The result is a genetic monstrosity – a VIP capable of only one expression: that of television self-presenters, people who always wear the same clothes, make the same gestures and have the same body language, whether they are in the North or the South, in Italy or somewhere else. You feel bound to compare these stereotypical zombies with the feast of gestures, feelings, seriousness, absurdity, spontaneity and theatricality which emerges from Gardin's photographs. Television hardly ever succeeds in discovering the world – instead, it „produces" it like a stage play, assigning everyone a role. As soon as a TV reporter shows his or her face, people in any village dress up to the nines, remove any last remaining blemishes, try to achieve a golden mean that suits a „folksy" stereotype, and finally appear like figures in a postcard. This process turns a local product into something exotic – any individuality is stylised into a bizarre spectacle.

In making people seem uninhibited, television also makes them seem insincere. They all have the same mechanical good humour or hostility about them. This applies whether  we are looking at a mayor extolling the virtues of his home patch, an ordinary woman interviewed in the street, a politician who pretends to be like you and me, a simple soul who imitates politicians' foibles, an intellectual or a footballer. When the recording is edited, any stammers or promises are taken out, or else stylised into a rhetorical end in themselves. What is left is a sort of waxworks' museum, an almighty yawn, a fancy menu without any bread.

„Bread" is always „on the table" in Berengo Gardin's photographs, which depict things that are simple yet different from region to region. Just compare these groups of people, their conversations, their isolation, with the sameness so evident in other media. In these photos, by contrast, we see people surrounded by air, smells, and atmosphere. Photography has a substance and depth all its own, which allow room for imagination. These pictures do not shut viewers out, but allow them access to what is going on inside. Every detail has its own specific significance. Here, we can see that a visual sensibility has been at work, a view of the world which does not „classify" people or things into a hierarchical structure, which is not trying to prove anything and which has no self-congratulatory „pictorial concept" behind it.

Whilst photography uses technique and lighting to good effect, it can also do with light being shed on it. Then we can see the full variety of North and South, of bandits and policemen, of workers and the middle class, of lonely isolation and collective celebration, of ostentation and modesty, all of which make up the richness of Italian life. When we look at industrial and rural landscapes, bustling cities and secluded villages, faces that reveal hard labour as well as boredom, and the major events of sacred rituals and political gatherings – we see a complex, productive country, rich in words, dialects and gestures.

So we see the policemen from *Pinocchio*, the dignified poverty of Toto and De Filippo, the *Salomé* of Bene, Fellini's beaches, Pasolini's periphery, we sense the silence of a Calvino or Sciascia. Before us we see spread out a country which comprises several lands, a multiplicity which the conformist vision of a videocentric age could never convey. As the son of a father from northern Italy and a mother from southern Italy, I see these photographs reflecting the landscapes and the souls I have known. They depict my childhood, my political past, my friends and enemies, my spontaneity and my flashes of wit. When we look at these pictures we feel strongly that we are not just Italians but also Albanians, Phoenicians, Germans, Slavs and Arabs. Italy has turned its face toward the Mediterranean, as is clear from the music of Fabrizio de André – the huge harbour soaks up the rumours and the songs that issue from all the myriad countries we call Italy.

First and foremost, Berengo Gardin's photographs resurrect the fundamental debate about our own tradition. On one side we have „I'm not sure you quite realise who you're dealing with" – a rather arrogant search for recognition, expressed over-rhetorically. On the other hand, we hear the battle-cry of Toto: „ma mi faccia il piacere" („Sorry, but I must insist") – an ironical turn of phrase which challenges any form of authority, formal structure, or system. In some of these pictures we look absurd, in others dignified, ugly, bored, conformist – but always willing to pull a face and laugh. We are something more than merely candidates for opinion research exercises or questionnaires on viewing figures. Gardin gives the Italians back their real faces – something which the conservatism of videocentricity has sacrificed to media exercises in „camera-friendly" beautification. Gardin reminds us that we have suffered – and still do suffer – poverty, emigration, hunger, and oppression; that we are – and remain – presumptuous, selfish, vulgar and talkative.

The seemingly contradictory qualities of uniqueness and variation are what keep the photos alive. We find the same qualities in De André, whose name I like to mention as he loved photography and described himself as a „mangiatore di facce", „someone who devours faces". Photography transforms and captures, isolates and selects. It grants us a moment of magic, an instant of reconstruction – the moment of its creation giving us room for imagination and comparison.

Such pauses for reflection are never possible on television, that quick-tempered tyrant which no longer has the courage to see the world as it is. Instead, it creates a substitute reality day after day, without ever emerging from its grandness or its dejection. Having said all this, let us not imagine that all still pictures have the variety and vitality of Gardin's photographs. There is a kind of photography that is more akin to special effects in the cinema. This „pseudo-photography" tries hard to spring surprises and be hypnotic, but it is incapable of creating dialogue or setting a narrative in motion.

We ourselves communicate with the pictures. And so we are free to read the truth and the emotions they contain – as well as the insincerity, the posing, the propaganda, the pointless virtuosity. But a word of warning: photographs have eyes, too. They remind us of real glances, of people both close to us and distant from us, of our past and present, as well as of things we have forgotten and never want to see again. Their prodigious profusion makes these photos a kind of critique of our world, however uncompromising or seductive we may find them. They also show us that „all the world's a stage", not just a faded stereotype we praise every day as a „new form of communication".

Looking at these pictures, we are struck by a penetrating gaze that has no fear of boredom or emotion, a vision that „confronts" its subjects head-on and in all sincerity. This results in a depth of recognition, a destiny, which defy the phrase-mongers and sophists who have turned their backs on pictures as such and now see the world only in terms of special effect pyrotechnic displays or sterile fact-sheets on viewing-figures. We seem to be living in a world which daily feeds us the illusion that now we can only know about distance, and are no longer capable of closeness. Both the craft and the art which Berengo Gardin shares with us in these pages tell us of his struggle to get close, of his own journeys, of a day in the life of a keen observer. All this is totally up-to-the-minute and it goes to make up the fruitful complexity from which we must never shrink.

Stefano Benni

## Ein Land – viele Länder

„Die Fotografie muss einer Anforderung gerecht werden, die sich in anderen Medien mit größerer Leichtigkeit oder Zynismus vertuschen oder verschleiern lässt: Ein Paradoxon soll sichtbar gemacht werden und beunruhigend wirken, das im Oszillieren der Kunstformen zwischen einem Höchstmaß an künstlerischer Gestaltung und einem Maximum an Wahrheitstreue besteht. Von der Fotografie wird erwartet – und darin gleicht sie der Alchemie –, dass sie die Bestandteile zeigt, so, als seien die Grundelemente von Gefühl, Instinkt und Gestik in anderen Formen der Kunst und Kommunikation nicht mehr erkennbar, da sie zu stark vermischt, zu verbraucht und korrumpiert sind. Die Fotografie soll die Reinheit eines Augenblicks festhalten, sie soll in der Art einer Felsspalte oder eines Fossils geologisch konservieren, also das bewahren, was die rasende Abfolge realer oder künstlicher Ereignisse in scheinbar gleichgültiger Geschwindigkeit sonst mit sich reißt."

Diese Zeilen schrieb ich vor einigen Jahren in der Einleitung zu einer Ausstellung junger Fotografen. Seither ist der Videozentrismus der italienischen Kultur noch steriler geworden. Ich habe die Welt von Berengo Gardin mit Erleichterung betreten, denn sie bestärkt mich in der Auffassung, dass wir das Fernsehen als „modern" und die Fotografie als „alt" bezeichnen, obwohl es doch häufig genau umgekehrt ist. Das Fernsehen ist konservativ, phrasenhaft und schreckt vor der Komplexität zurück. Die Fotografie ist neugierig, deckt auf und spürt nach. Ich spreche hier nicht von der tödlichen Monotonie der Modefotografien oder von den pseudo-innovativen Werbeaufnahmen, die nicht zufällig in einer symbiotischen Beziehung zum Fernsehen stehen. Ich meine vielmehr die Fotografie, die Bilder hervorbringt, denen noch das „Staunen" innewohnt. Jeder Bildband, ob professionell oder nicht, scheint mir abwechslungsreicher zu sein als ein solches Palimpsest. Wenn wir den Fernseher einschalten, dann sehen wir auf allen Kanälen die selben Gesichter. Es handelt sich dabei um einen morbiden Stammesritus, eine unselige Selbstbefruchtung, und sie hat ein genetisch monströses Wesen hervorgebracht: den VIP, der nur einen einzigen Ausdruck kennt, nämlich den eines Menschen, der durch die Fernsehkamera gesehen wird, der sich auf die immer gleiche Art kleidet, gebärdet und bewegt, im Norden wie im Süden, in Italien und andernorts. Man kommt gar nicht umhin, diese stereotypen Zombies zu kontrastieren mit dem Fest an Gesten, Gefühlen, Ernsthaftigkeit, Lächerlichkeit, Spontaneität und Theatralik, das durch die Fotografien Gardins ins Licht gerückt wird. Dem Fernsehen gelingt es fast nie, die Welt zu entdecken, stattdessen inszeniert es sie und schreibt jedem seine Rolle vor. Bei Ankunft des Fernsehreporters wirft sich jedes Dorf in Schale, korrigiert die letzten Schönheitsfehler, sucht eine folkloristische goldene Mitte und erscheint schließlich wie auf einer Ansichtskarte. Das lokale Produkt wird exotisch, jede Eigenheit wird zum bizarren Spektakel stilisiert.

Das Fernsehen hat die Menschen unbefangen und zugleich falsch werden lassen, alle haben die gleiche Gestik, die gleiche aufgesetzte Heiterkeit oder Streitbarkeit an sich: der Bürgermeister, der die Vorzüge seines Ortes aufzählt ebenso wie die Frau, die auf der Straße interviewt wird, die Politiker, die sich als Menschen wie du und ich ausgeben wie die einfachen Menschen, welche die Ticks der Politiker nachahmen und der Intellektuelle genau wie der Fußballer. Beim Filmschnitt werden das Stottern und die Versprecher herausgefiltert oder zum rhetorischen Selbstzweck stilisiert. Was bleibt, ist ein Wachsfigurenkabinett, ein großes Gähnen, ein reiches italienisches Menü, dem etwas Wesentliches fehlt: das Brot.

In den Fotografien Berengo Gardins ist das „Brot" nicht vergessen, denn sie zeigen, was einfach ist, aber in jeder Region unterschiedlich. Vergleichen Sie diese Gruppen von Menschen, diese Gespräche, diese Einsamkeit mit der Gleichförmigkeit in anderen Medien. In diesen Bildern sind die Personen von Luft, Gerüchen und Atmosphäre umgeben. Die Fotografie hat eine eigene Substanz und Tiefe, in der Raum für Phantasie bleibt. Das Bild schließt den Betrachter nicht aus, sondern erlaubt ihm den Zutritt zur Szene. Jede Einzelheit hat Ihre spezifische Bedeutung – hier war die Sensibilität eines Auges am Werke, ein Blick, der nicht in Hierarchien „einordnet", der nichts beweisen will und hinter dem kein selbstgefälliges Bildkonzept steht.

Die Fotografie benutzt Technik und Licht, kann aber auch selbst wieder beleuchtet werden. Und so sehen wir die Vielfalt von Nord und Süd, von Räubern und Gendarmen, von Arbeiterschaft und Bourgeoisie, von Einsamkeit und ländlichen Festen, von Geltungssucht und Bescheidenheit, die den geheimnisvollen Reichtum Italiens ausmacht. Wenn wir die industriellen und ländlichen Gebiete, die Metropolen und die Stille der Dörfer, die Gesichter von Arbeit und Langeweile, die großen Inszenierungen der sakralen Riten und der politischen Veranstaltungen betrachten, dann zeigt sich uns ein kompliziertes und fruchtbares Land, reich an Worten, an Dialekten und Gesten.

Da gibt es die Gendarmen aus *Pinocchio*, die würdevolle Armut bei - Totò und De Filippo, die *Salome* von Bene, die fellinischen Strände, die passolinische Peripherie, wir empfinden die Stille eines Calvino oder Sciascia. Vor uns ausgebreitet ist ein Land, das viele Länder umfasst, eine Vielfalt, die der konformistische Videozentrismus nicht zeigen würde. Für mich, der ich der Sohn eines norditalienischen Vaters und einer süditalienischen Mutter bin, spiegeln diese Fotografien die Landschaften und die Seelen wider, meine Kindheit, meine politische Vergangenheit, meine Freunde und Feinde, meine Spontaneität und meine Gewitztheit. Bei ihrer Betrachtung spüren wir, dass wir nicht nur Italiener sind, sondern auch Albaner, Phönizier, Deutsche, Slawen und Araber. Das Gesicht Italiens ist dem Mittelmeer zugewandt, so wie man es in der Musik von Fabrizio de André findet: Der große Hafen empfängt die Gerüchte und die Lieder aus den vielen Ländern, die wir Italien nennen.

Die Fotografien Berengo Gardins rufen vor allem den grundlegenden Dialog über unsere eigene Tradition wieder ins Leben. Auf der einen Seite steht das „Sie wissen wohl nicht, wen Sie hier vor sich haben", die Geltungssucht, die übertriebene Rhetorik, auf der anderen Seite der Kampfruf von Totò „ma mi faccia il piacere", „aber ich muss doch sehr bitten", eine ironische Redewendung, die jede Autorität, jede Formgebung oder jedes Schema in Frage stellt. Auf diesen Bildern erscheinen wir komisch, doch manchmal mit Würde, hässlich, aber echt, gelangweilt und konformistisch, aber sofort bereit, uns zu verstellen und zu lachen. Wir sind nicht nur Kandidaten für Meinungsumfragen oder Einschaltquoten. Gardin gibt den Italienern wieder ein Gesicht – der konservative Videozentrismus hat es der Schönmacherei der Medien geopfert. Er erinnert uns daran, dass wir arm, emigriert, ausgehungert und geduckt waren (und bleiben) und dass wir anmaßend, egoistisch, ordinär und geschwätzig sind (und bleiben).

Diese Einzigartigkeit und Vielfalt sind genau das, was die Bilder bewahren. Wie bei De André, an den ich gerne erinnere, weil er die Fotografie liebte und sich als „Mangiatore di facce", als einen „Gesichterfresser" bezeichnete. Die Fotografie verändert und hält fest, isoliert und wählt aus. Sie gewährt die magische Zeit, den Moment zu rekonstruieren, in dem sie entstand, sie gibt Raum für Phantasie und Vergleiche.

Diese Zeit gewährt das Fernsehen nicht, dieser jähzornige, alte Tyrann, der nicht mehr den Mut aufbringt, die Welt so zu sehen wie sie ist, sondern sie stattdessen jeden Tag simuliert, ohne dadurch auch nur einen Schritt aus seiner Grandiosität oder Depression herauszutreten. Doch besitzen nicht alle Bilder diese Vielfalt, diese Vitalität. Es gibt eine Art der Fotografie, die eher dem special effect im Kino vergleichbar ist. Sie will überraschen und hypnotisieren, sie vermag aber keinen Dialog herzustellen und erzählt auch nichts. Wir sind es, die mit den Bildern kommunizieren, es steht uns frei, die Wahrheit und die Emotionen herauszulesen, aber auch die Falschheit, die Posen, die Propaganda, die nutzlose Virtuosität. Doch Vorsicht: Auch Fotos haben Augen. Sie erinnern uns an wirkliche Blicke, an uns nahe und ferne Menschen, an unsere Vergangenheit und unsere Gegenwart sowie an Dinge, die wir vergessen haben und nicht wieder sehen möchten. Die Bilder sind in ihrer wunderbaren Vielfalt eine Beurteilung für uns, so unerbittlich und verführerisch sie auch sein mögen, und sie zeigen uns, dass dies hier das Welttheater ist und nicht der miserable Abklatsch, den wir täglich als „neue Kommunikation" preisen. Uns trifft ein durchdringender Blick, der keine Benommenheit und kein Gefühl fürchtet, sondern sich mit Wahrhaftigkeit vor sein Motiv „schiebt" – eine Erkenntnis, ein Schicksal, das den Phrasendreschern und Sophisten trotzt, die sich von den Bildern abgewandt haben und die Welt nur noch durch das Feuerwerk eines special effects oder durch die Sterilität eines Zahlenschemas sehen können. Es scheint, dass wir in einer Welt, in der jeden Tag die Illusion vermittelt wird, über die Entfernung hinweg informiert zu sein, nicht mehr zur Nähe fähig sind. Das Handwerk und die Kunst von Berengo Gardin erzählen uns von der Anstrengung, sich zu nähern, von solchen Reisen, von einem Alltag des Beobachtens. Das ist modern, das ist die fruchtbare Komplexität, vor der wir nicht zurückweichen dürfen.

Stefano Benni

# Biography

Gianni Berengo Gardin was born on 10th October 1930 in Santa Margherita Ligure. After living for some time in Switzerland, Rome, Paris and Venice, he settled in Milan. In 1954 he first took up photography. His first photo-report appeared in the weekly *Il Mondo*, with whose editor, Mario Pannunzio, he collaborated until 1965. He has been a professional photographer since 1962. Berengo Gardin has worked for leading Italian and international publications, and has published over 180 pictorial books. Some 70 exhibitions, in Italy and other countries, have been devoted to his work. These include Arles in 1987, Milan in 1990, Lausanne in 1991, and Paris, in 1990 and 1997. His latest exhibition took place in 1999 in the Leica Gallery, New York.

His photographs have also been shown in the „Photokina" in Cologne, at „Expo" in Montreal, and at Venice Biennales.

His pictures have been exhibited in several museums and cultural institutions – including the Calcografia Nazionale in Rome, the Museum of Modern Art, New York, and the Bibliothèque Nationale as well as the Maison Européenne de la Photographie in Paris, the Eastman House, Rochester, N.Y., the Musée de l'Elysée, Lausanne, and the Museum of Aesthetic Art, Beijing.

In 1972 the magazine *Modern Photography* featured him as one of „the World's Top 32 Photographers". In 1975 Cecil Beaton mentioned him in his book *The Magic Image. The Genius of Photography from 1839 to the Present Day*. Also in 1975 Bill Brandt selected him for the exhibition „Twentieth Century Landscape Photographs" at the V&A (Victoria and Albert Museum), London. In his book *The Image and the Eye* (Oxford 1982), he is the only photographer to be mentioned by Ernst H. Gombrich. In his history of Italian photography, Italo Zannier calls him the „leading postwar photographer".

In 1981 Gardin was awarded the Scanno Prize as the best photographer of the year for his volume *India dei Villaggi*. In 1990 he was guest-of-honour at the „Mois de la Foto" in Paris, at which he was awarded the Brassai Prize. In 1995, at the Rencontres Internationales de la Photographie in Arles, he was given the Leica Oskard Barnak Award, and in 1998 he was honoured with the Oscar Goldoni Prize as the best photographer of the year for *Zingari*.

## Biografie

Gianni Berengo Gardin wurde am 10. Oktober 1930 in Santa Margherita Ligure geboren. Nachdem er einige Zeit in der Schweiz, in Rom, Paris und Venedig gelebt hattte, ließ er sich in Mailand nieder. 1954 beschäftigte er sich zum ersten Mal mit Fotografie. Seine erste Bildreportage erschien in der Wochenzeitschrift *Il Mondo*, mit deren Leiter Mario Pannunzio er bis 1965 zusammenarbeitete. Seit 1962 ist er Berufsfotograf.

Berengo Gardin hat mit der Spitze der italienischen und internationalen Presse zusammengearbeitet und über 180 Bildbände veröffentlicht. Seinem Werk waren in Italien und in anderen Ländern rund 70 Austellungen gewidmet, unter anderem 1987 in Arles, 1990 in Mailand, 1991 in Lausanne sowie 1990 und 1997 in Paris. Die jüngste Ausstellung fand 1999 in der New Yorker Leica Gallery statt. Darüber hinaus wurden seine Werke auf der „Photokina" in Köln, der „Expo" in Montreal und den „Biennalen" in Venedig gezeigt.

Seine Bilder werden in vielen Museen und Kulturstiftungen gezeigt, beispielsweise in der Calcografia Nazionale in Rom, im Museum of Modern Art in New York, in der Bibliothèque National und der Maison Européenne de la Photographie in Paris, im Eastman House in Rochester (N.Y), im Musée de l'Elysée in Lausanne und im Museum of Aesthetic Art in Peking.

1972 führte die Zeitschrift *Modern Photography* ihn unter den „32 World's Top Photographers". 1975 erwähnt ihn Cecil Beaton in seinem Buch *The Magic Image. The Genius of Photography from 1839 to the Present Day*. 1975 wählt Bill Brandt ihn für die Ausstellung *Twentieth Century Landscape Photographs* im Victoria and Albert Museum in London aus. Ernst H. Gombrich nennt ihn als einzigen Fotografen in seinem Buch *The Image and the Eye* (Oxford 1982). In seiner Geschichte der italienischen Fotografie bezeichnet Italo Zannier ihn als den „bedeutendsten Fotografen der Nachkriegszeit".

1981 gewinnt er den Scanno-Preis als bester Fotograf des Jahres für den Band *India dei Villaggi*. 1990 ist er Ehrengast bei Mois de la Foto in Paris, wo er mit dem Brassaï-Preis ausgezeichnet wird. 1995 wird er bei den Rencontres Internationales de la Photographie in Arles mit dem Leica Oskard Barnak Award geehrt und 1998 als bester Fotograf des Jahres für *Zingari a Palermo* mit dem Oscar Goldoni Preis.

**Important works**

*Venise des Saison,* Paris 1965. *Toscane,* Lausanne 1967. *Morire di classe* (together with Carla Cerati, edited by Franco Basaglia, Turin 1969. *L'occhio come mestiere,* Milan 1970. *Un paese vent'anni dopo* (mit Cesare Zavattini), Turin 1976. *Dentro le case* (together with Luciano D'Alessandro), Milan 1977. *Gran Bretagna,* Milan 1977. *Dentro il Lavoro* (together with Luciano D'Alessandro), Milan 1978. *Case contadine,* Milan 1979. *India dei villaggi,* Venice 1980. *Spazi dell'uomo,* Ivrea 1980. *Gianni Berengo Gardin,* Milan 1982. *Archeologia industriale,* Milan 1983. „Il Mondo", Milan 1985. *Donne,* Rome 1989. *Gianni Berengo Gardin. Fotografie 1953–1990,* Udine 1990. *Lo studio di Giorgio Morandi,* Milan 1993. *Gli anni di Venezia,* Milan 1994. *La disperata allegria. Vivere da zingari a Firenze,* Florence, 1994. *Gianni Berengo Gardin. Immigini inedite 1954–1994,* Brescia 1995. *Foto Piano,* Rome 1996. *Zingari a Palermo. Herdelesi e Santa Rosalia,* Rome 1997. *Les Italiens 1953–1997,* Paris 1998. *Una città una fabbrica: Ivrea e la Olivetti,* Ivrea 1998.

**Wichtige Werke**

*Venise des Saison,* Paris 1965. *Toscane,* Lausanne 1967. *Morire di classe* (gemeinsam mit Carla Cerati, herausgegeben von Franco Basaglia, Turin 1969. *L'occhio come mestiere,* Mailand 1970. *Un paese vent'anni dopo* (mit Cesare Zavattini), Turin 1976. *Dentro le case* (mit Luciano D'Alessandro), Mailand 1977. *Gran Bretagna,* Mailand 1977. *Dentro il Lavoro* (mit Luciano D'Alessandro), Mailand 1978. *Case contadine,* Mailand 1979. *India dei villaggi,* Venedig 1980. *Spazi dell''uomo,* Ivrea 1980. Gianni Berengo Gardin, Mailand 1982. *Archeologia industriale,* Mailand 1983. „Il Mondo", Mailand 1985. *Donne,* Rom 1989. *Gianni Berengo Gardin. Fotografie 1953–1990,* Udine 1990. *Lo studio di Giorgio Morandi,* Mailand 1993. *Gli anni di Venezia,* Mailand 1994. *La disperata allegria. Vivere da zingari a Firenze,* Florenz, 1994. *Gianni Berengo Gardin. Immigini inedite 1954–1994,* Brescia 1995. Foto Piano, Rom 1996. *Zingari a Palermo. Herdelesi e Santa Rosalia,* Rom 1997. *Les Italiens 1953–1997,* Paris 1998. *Una città una fabbrica: Ivrea e la Olivetti,* Ivrea 1998.

# Photographs

# Bildteil

## 1950–1959

**24** Tuscany / Toskana, 1958
**25** Apulia / Apulien, 1958
**26** Apulia / Apulien, 1958
**27** Apulia / Apulien, 1959
**28** Apulia / Apulien, 1959
**29** Friuli / Friaul, 1958
**30** Ortisei, 1957
**31** Dolomites / Dolomiten, 1957
**32** Ortisei, 1957
**33** Venice: Lido / Venedig: Lido, 1958
**34** Venice: Lido / Venedig: Lido, 1958
**35** Apulia / Apulien, 1954
**36** Naples / Neapel, 1958
**37** Naples / Neapel, 1960
**38** Naples / Neapel, 1960
**39** Naples / Neapel, 1958
**40** Naples / Neapel, 1960
**41** Naples: District of Forcella / Neapel: Stadtteil Forcella, 1960
**42** Milan / Mailand, 1959
**43** Milan / Mailand, 1960
**44** Milan / Mailand, 1953
**45** Milan / Mailand, 1959
**46** Tuscany / Toskana, 1954
**47** Venice / Venedig, 1958
**48** Rome / Rom, 1958
**49** Venice / Venedig, 1958
**50** Venice: Film-extras / Venedig: Filmkomparsen, 1956
**51** Rome / Rom: Piazza San Pietro, 1959
**52** Venice / Venedig, 1960
**53** Venice / Venedig, 1960
**54** Venice: Traditional regatta / Venedig: Historische Regatta, 1958
**55** Venice / Venedig, 1958
**56** Venice / Venedig, 1962
**57** Venice: Procession on the Piazza San Marco / Venedig: Prozession auf der Piazza San Marco, 1960
**58** Venice: in a vaporetto / Venedig: Im Vaporetto, 1960
**59** Venice / Venedig, 1958
**60** Venice / Venedig, 1957
**61** Venice / Venedig, 1957
**62** Venice / Venedig, 1960
**63** Venice: A wedding in Santa Maria del Giglio / Venedig: Hochzeit in Santa Maria del Giglio, 1958
**64** Venice / Venedig, 1958
**65** Venice / Venedig, 1956
**66** Venice / Venedig, 1960
**67** Venice / Venedig, 1957
**68** Venice: Lido / Venedig: Lido, 1958
**69** Venice: Lido / Venedig: Lido, 1959
**70** Venice: Lido / Venedig: Lido, 1958
**71** Venice / Venedig, 1959

## 1960–1969

**74** Apulia / Apulien, 1966
**75** Tuscany / Toskana, 1965
**76** Apulia / Apulien, 1965
**77** Veneto / Venetien, 1966
**78** Friuli / Friaul, 1960
**79** Friuli / Friaul, 1963
**80** Tuscany / Toskana, 1965
**81** South Tyrol / Südtirol, 1967
**82** Sardinia / Sardinien, 1968
**83** Sardinia / Sardinien, 1970
**84** Sardinia / Sardinien, 1968
**85** Abruzzen, 1969
**86** Calabria / Kalabrien, 1966
**87** Calabria / Kalabrien, 1966
**88** Calabria / Kalabrien, 1967
**89** Assisi, 1968
**90** Ivrea, 1968
**91** Veneto / Venetien, 1969
**92** Oriolo Romano, 1965
**93** Oriolo Romano, 1965
**94** Molise, 1969
**95** Basilicata, 1966
**96** Irsina, 1966
**97** Messina, 1966
**98** Sardinia / Sardinien, 1968
**99** Sardinia / Sardinien, 1968
**100** Apulia / Apulien, 1966
**101** Milan / Mailand, 1967
**102** Assisi, 1968
**103** Milan / Mailand, 1960
**104** Sotto il Monte, 1969

## 1970–1979

**180** Le Marche / Marken, 1976
**181** Luzzara, 1973
**182** Turin, 1971
**183** Treviso, 1975
**184** Luzzara, 1973
**185** Luzzara, 1973
**186** Florence / Florenz, 1971
**187** Siena, 1976
**188** Perugia, 1976
**189** Luzzara, 1973
**190** Veneto / Venetien, 1976
**191** Luzzara, 1974
**192** Bagheria, 1977
**193** Rome: People turned out of their homes,
on the Piazza San Giovanni /
Rom: Ausquartierte auf der Piazza
San Giovanni, 1977
**194** Milan / Mailand, 1975
**195** Rome / Rom, 1974
**196** Milan / Mailand, 1971
**197** Milan / Mailand, 1971
**198** Milan / Mailand, 1971
**199** Milan / Mailand, 1971
**200** Milan / Mailand, 1970
**201** Milan / Mailand, 1971
**202** Milan, Emigrant / Mailand, Emigrant, 1970
**203** Milan, Emigrant / Mailand, Emigrant, 1976
**204** Milan, Emigrant / Mailand, Emigrant, 1976
**205** Milan, Emigrant / Mailand, Emigrant, 1976
**206** Monfalcone, 1977
**207** Monfalcone, 1970
**208** Modena, Ferrari, 1978
**209** Turin, Fiat, 1978
**210** Turin, Fiat, 1978
**211** Turin, Fiat, 1978
**212** Ivrea, Olivetti, 1977
**213** Ivrea, Olivetti, 1977
**214** Ivrea, Olivetti, 1974
**215** Ivrea, Olivetti, 1970
**216** Milan / Mailand, 1975
**217** Rome / Rom, 1978
**218** Turin, 1972
**219** Perugia, 1977
**220** Turin: Moonlighting /
Schwarzarbeit, 1976

**221** Milan / Mailand, 1971
**222** Calabria / Kalabrien, 1976
**223** Friuli / Friaul, 1970
**224** Udine, 1970
**225** Valle Padana / Poebene, 1977
**226** Vercelli, 1972
**227** Vercelli, 1972
**228** Calabria / Kalabrien, 1978
**229** Otranto, 1979
**230** Luzzara, Cesare Zavattini, 1974
**231** Luzzara, 1974
**232** Luzzara, 1973
**233** Luzzara, 1974
**234** Luzzara, 1973
**235** Luzzara, 1973
**236** Luzzara, 1973
**237** Varese, 1974
**233** Friuli / Friaul, 1976
**239** Friuli / Friaul, 1976
**240** Caserta, 1975
**241** Naples / Neapel, 1978
**242** Assisi, 1976
**243** Assisi, 1975
**244** Umbria / Umbrien, 1978
**245** Assisi, 1976
**248** Luzzara, 1973
**247** Assisi, 1976
**248** Gubbio, 1975
**249** Umbria / Umbrien, 1978.
**250** Rome / Rom, 1975
**251** Ivrea, 1974
**252** Friuli / Friaul, 1970
**253** Friuli / Friaul, 1970
**254** Milan / Mailand, 1975
**255** Rome / Rom, 1974
**256** Calabria / Kalabrien, 1976
**257** Luzzara, 1973
**258** Sardinia: House where Gramsci was born /
Sardinien, Geburtshaus von Gramsci,
1976
**259** Milan: Occupation of the Università
Statale /
Mailand: Besetzung der Università Statale,
1971
**260** Siena, 1972
**261** Assisi: Monastery enclosure /
Klausurkonvent, 1972

**1980–1989**

**333** Orvieto, 1985
**334** Pavia, 1988
**335** Scanno, 1986
**336** Sicily / Sizilien, 1987
**337** Rome / Rom, 1985
**338** Pompei, 1988
**339** Rome / Rom, 1988
**340** Rome / Rom, 1984
**341** Milan: Opening of the fair /
 Mailand: Eröffnung der Messe, 1985
**342** Campania / Kampanien, 1984
**343** Liguria / Ligurien, 1984
**344** Milan / Mailand, 1984
**345** Milan / Mailand, 1988
**346** Rome / Rom, 1987
**347** Ivrea, 1990
**348** Milan / Mailand, 1986
**349** Genoa / Genua, 1988
**350** Naples / Neapel, 1981
**351** Naples / Neapel. 1981
**352** Genoa / Genua, 1988
**353** Venice / Venedig, 1987
**354** Milan, ca. 1980 / Mailand, etwa 1980
**355** Trieste / Triest, 1984
**356** Sesto San Giovanni, 1986
**357** Genoa / Genua, 1983
**358** Genoa / Genua, 1988
**359** Genoa / Genua, 1988
**360** Marghera, 1981
**361** Genoa / Genua, 1992

**1990–1999**

**364** Emilia, 1992
**365** Milan / Mailand, 1994
**366** Padua, 1995
**367** Trieste / Triest, 1998
**368** Rome / Rom, 1995
**369** Trieste / Triest, 1998
**370** Bolzano / Bozen, 1995
**371** Cervia, 1990
**372** Naples / Neapel, 1997
**373** Montecatini, 1992
**374** Sicily / Sizilien 1995
**375** Milan–Rome / Mailand–Rom, 1991
**376** Milan–Rome / Mailand–Rom, 1991

**377** Milan–Rome / Mailand–Rom, 1991
**378** Pilgrimage to Loreto /
 Wallfahrt nach Loreto, 1995
**379** Pilgrimage to Loreto /
 Wallfahrt nach Loreto, 1995
**380** Loreto, 1994
**381** Alberobello, 1994
**382** Alberobello, 1995
**383** Sciacca, 1994
**384** Alberobello, 1994
**385** Campobasso, 1991
**386** Trapani, 1987
**387** Trapani, 1991
**388** Sicily / Sizilien, 1991
**389** Sicily / Sizilien, 1991
**390** Taranto, 1993
**391** Sicily / Sizilien, 1990
**392** Genoa / Genua, 1997
**393** Milan / Mailand, 1997
**394** Turin, 1998
**395** Milan / Mailand, 1998
**396** Rome / Rom, 1992
**397** Rome / Rom, 1992
**398** Bologna, 1998
**399** Rome / Rom, 1991
**400** Bolzano / Bozen, 1995
**401** Bolzano / Bozen, 1995
**402** Rome / Rom, 1997
**403** Rome / Rom, 1997
**404** Umbria: Earthquake /
 Umbrien: Erdbeben, 1998
**405** Umbria: Earthquake /
 Umbrien: Erdbeben, 1998
**406** Lombardy / Lombardei, 1998
**407** Lombardy / Lombardei, 1998
**408** Rome / Rom, 1993
**409** Modena, 1994
**410** Modena, 1994
**411** Modena, 1994
**412** Modena, 1994
**413** Modena, 1994
**414** Modena, 1994
**415** Alberobello, 1997
**416** Lombardy / Lombardei, 1992
**417** Lombardy / Lombardei, 1992
**418** San Marino, 1997
**419** Gorizia, 1995

**420** Milan / Mailand, 1997
**421** Milan / Mailand, 1997
**422** Vercelli, 1998
**423** Vercelli, 1991
**424** Vercelli, 1998
**425** Vercelli, 1998
**426** Vercelli, 1996
**427** Vercelli, 1998
**428** Vercelli, 1998
**429** Vercelli, 1998
**430** Le Marche / Marken, 1991
**431** Le Marche / Marken, 1991
**432** Rome / Rom, 1992
**433** Naples / Neapel, 1997
**434** Le Marche / Marken, 1991
**435** Le Marche / Marken, 1991
**436** Bologna, 1997
**437** Turin, 1995
**438** Pordenone, 1998
**439** Pordenone, 1998
**440** Alberobello, 1997
**441** Imperia, 1993
**442** Capri, 1995
**443** Gulf of Naples / Golf von Neapel: 1995
**444** Lago Maggiore, 1993
**445** Islands, Tremiti / Tremiti-Inseln: 1995
**446** Palermo: Camp-site of non-residents /
Lagerplatz von Nichtsesshaften, 1995
**447** Florence: Camp-site of non-residents /
Florenz: Lagerplatz von Nichtsesshaften,
1993
**448** Palermo: Camp-site of non-residents /
Lagerplatz von Nichtsesshaften, 1995
**449** Florence: Camp-site of non-residents /
Florenz: Lagerplatz von Nichtsesshaften,
1993
**450** Palermo: Camp-site of non-residents /
Lagerplatz von Nichtsesshaften, 1995
**451** Florence: Camp-site of non-residents /
Florenz: Lagerplatz von Nichtsesshaften,
1993
**452** Palermo: Camp-site of non-residents /
Lagerplatz von Nichtsesshaften, 1996
**453** Palermo: Camp-site of non-residents /
Lagerplatz von Nichtsesshaften, 1995
**454** Bolzano / Bozen, 1995
**455** Alberobello, 1993

**456** Marengo, 1994
**457** Marengo, 1994
**458** Veneto / Venetien, 1998
**459** Veneto / Venetien, 1998
**460** Sciacca, 1994
**461** Sciacca, 1994
**462** Bolzano / Bozen, 1995
**463** Rome / Rom, 1994
**464** Umbertide, 1995
**465** Trieste / Triest, 1998
**466** Linosa, 1991
**467** Linosa, 1991
**468** Cagliari, 1995
**469** Cagliari, 1995
**470** Bolzano / Bozen, 1995
**471** Rome / Rom, 1995
**472** Pavia, 1997
**473** Bolzano / Bozen, 1995
**474** Pavia, 1997
**475** Parma, 1997
**476** Parma, 1997
**477** Milan / Mailand: Dario Fo, 1995

**1950-1959**

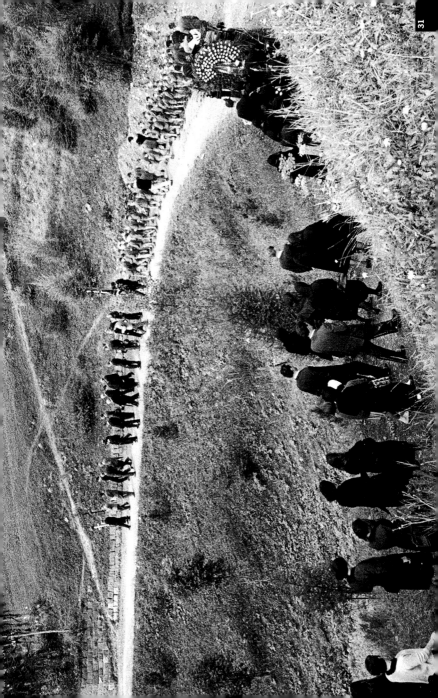

**1960-1969**

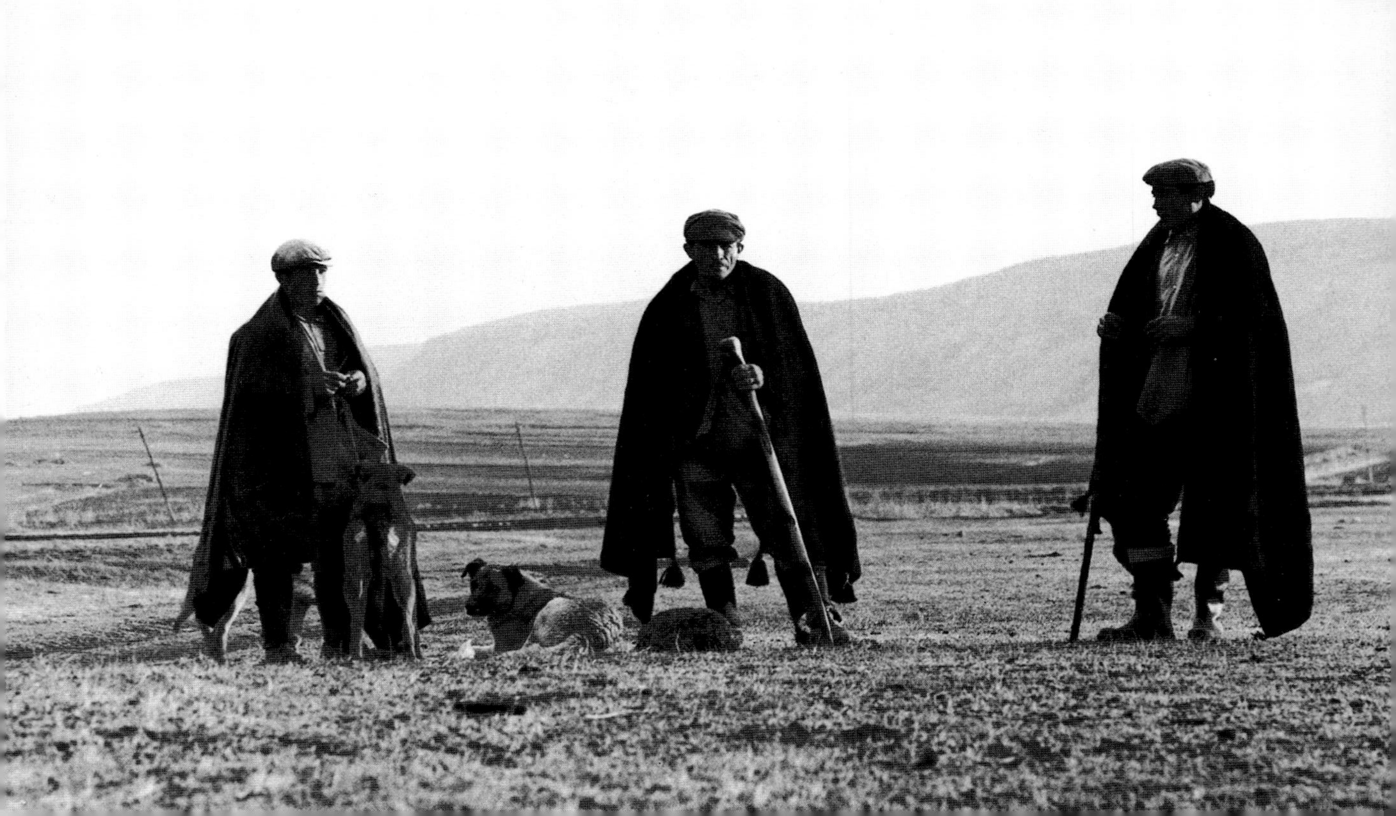

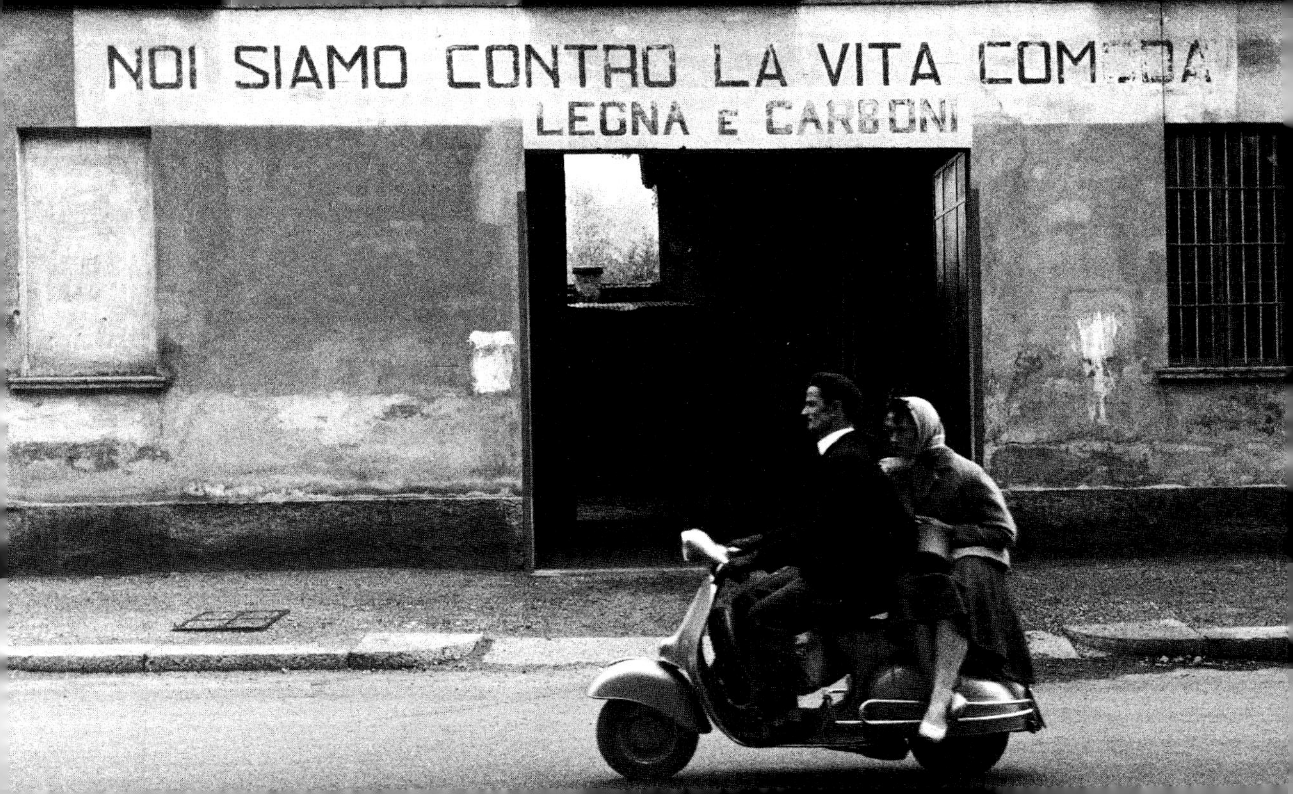
NOI SIAMO CONTRO LA VITA COM
LEGNA E CARBONI

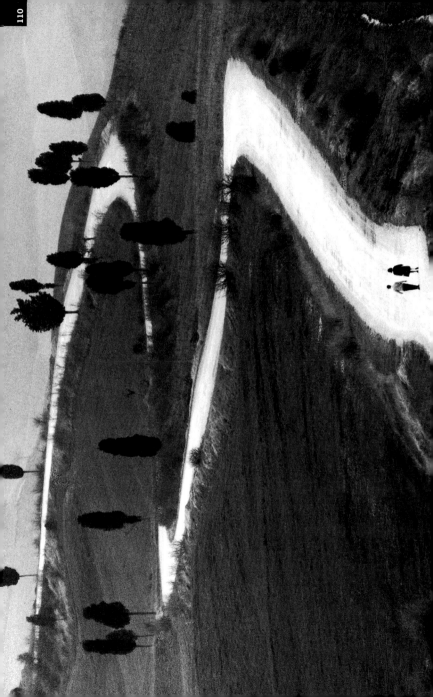

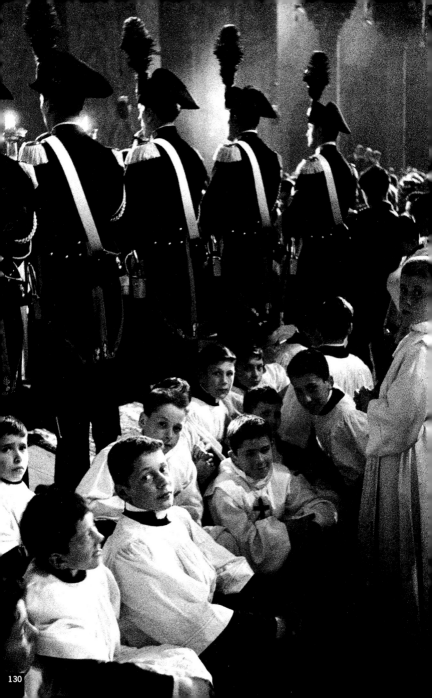

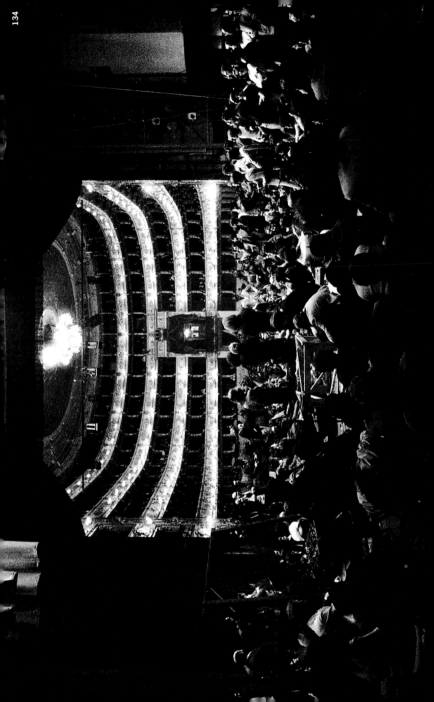

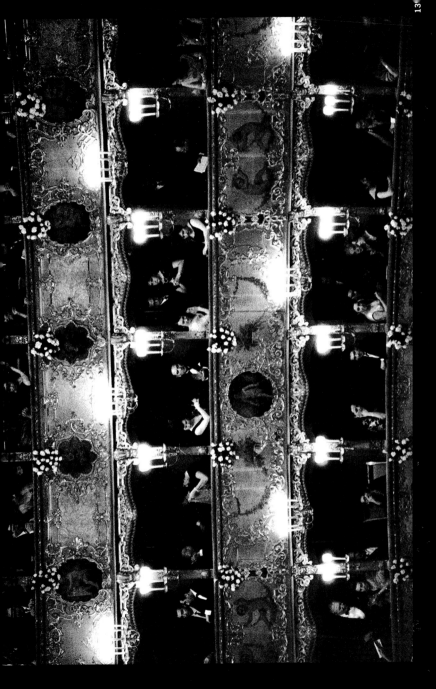

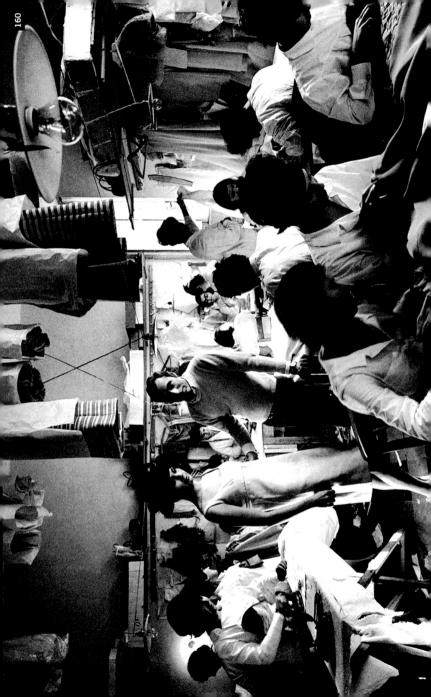

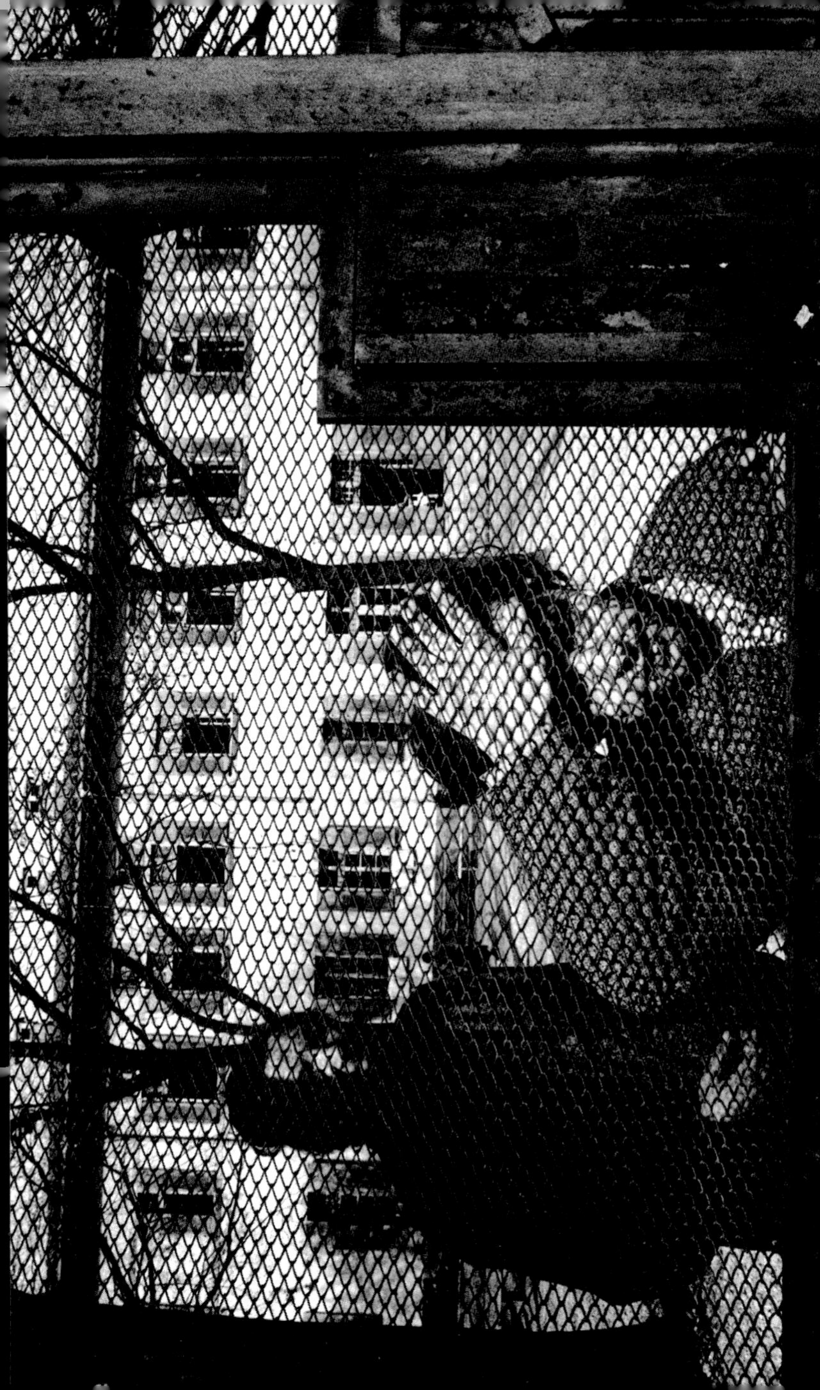

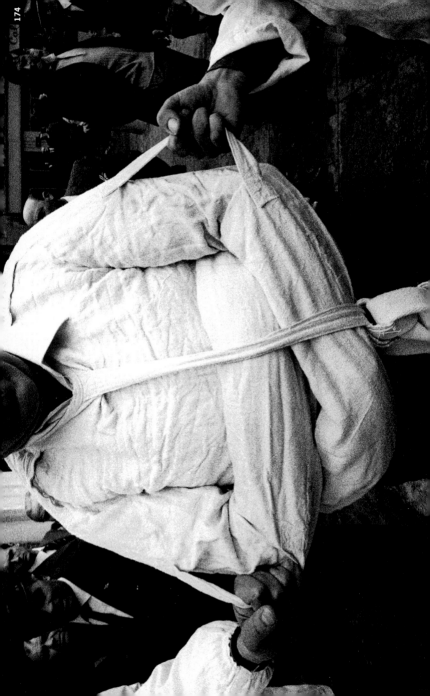

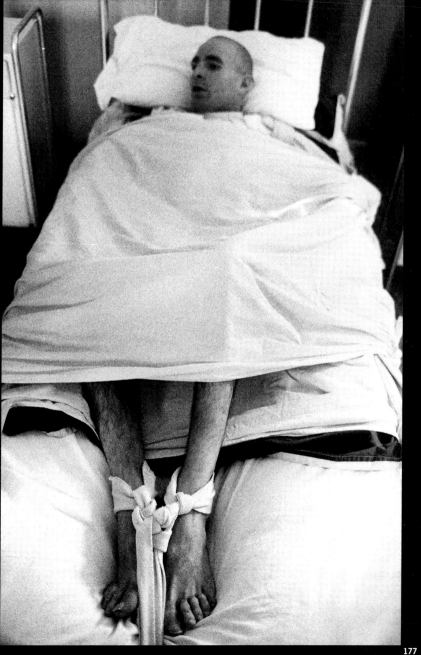

**1970-1979**

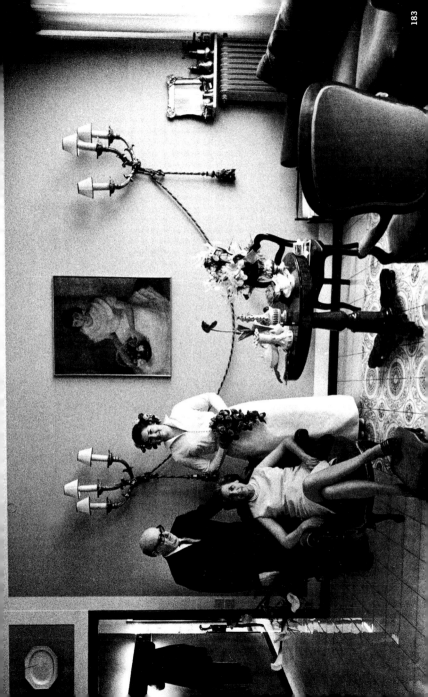

## NON E' UNA TROVATA PUBBLICITARIA!

... ne e l'immagine
... iono sull'astuccio
... mai famosa PASTA
... ANO, il dentifricio
... splendore ai d...
... n'invenzione o...
... ubblicitaria, ma...
... riproduce fe...
... ionomia del...
... e Ciccarelli, a...
... in una fotogr...
... gli Emilia, N...
... punto è la...
... dovinata, di...
... ricio diffuso
... ndo per la
... acia.
... Maddalena
... armacie
... se
... ugante L. 4...
... rande L. 3...

PASTA
"C...

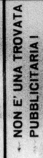

UOMO

PASTA

### NON E' UNA TROVATA PUBBLICITARIA !

Il nome e l'immagine che
compaio... tuccio d...
la ormai ...STA
CAPITAN ...frici...
dona lo ... re ai
non sono u... zione c...
trovata ...
confez... e
ment...
tor C
ra c...
dell...
glie...
soin, e...
cetta,
Maria.
ttimo
...tutt...
...ont...
In t...
citt...

Tub...

...de

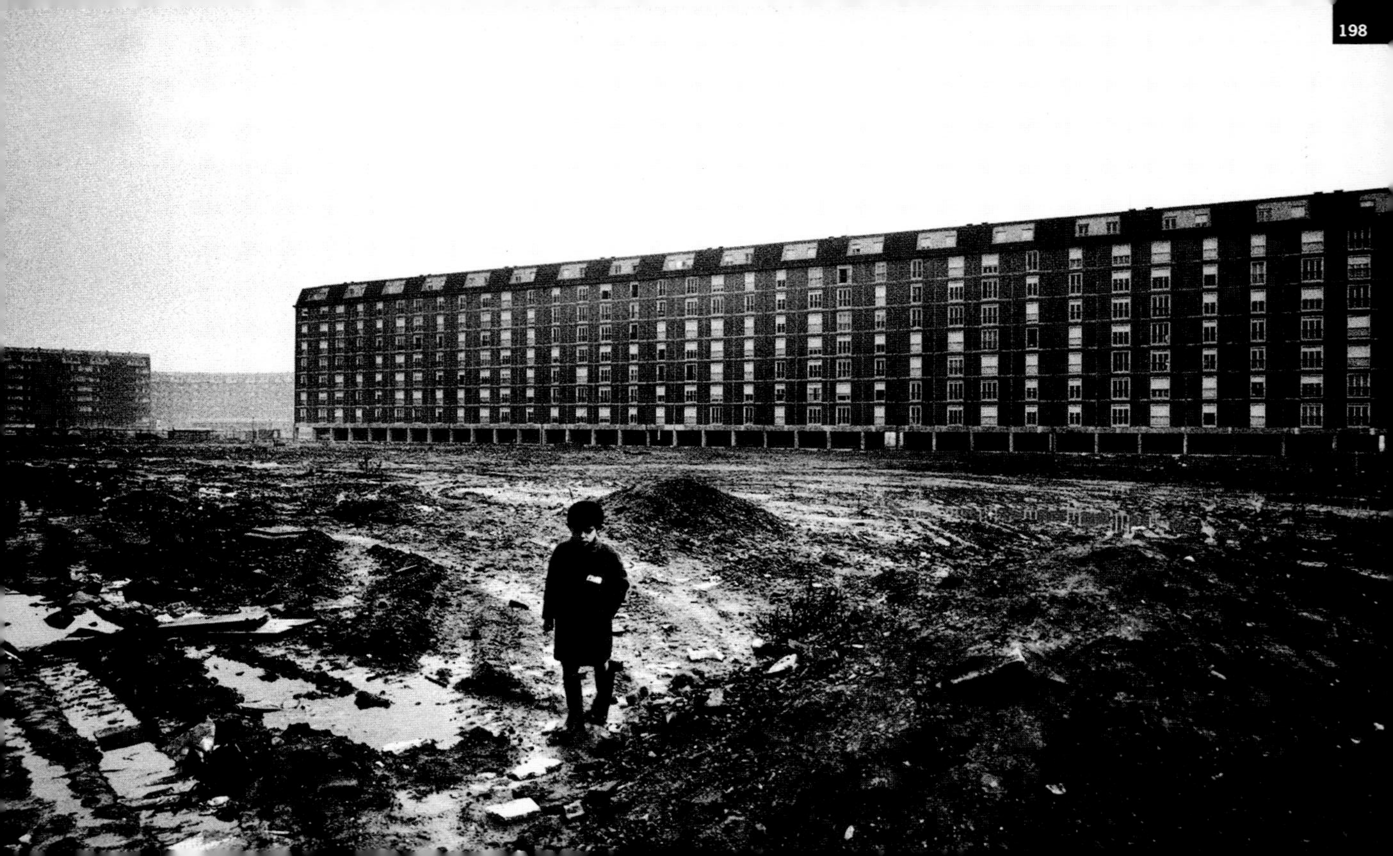

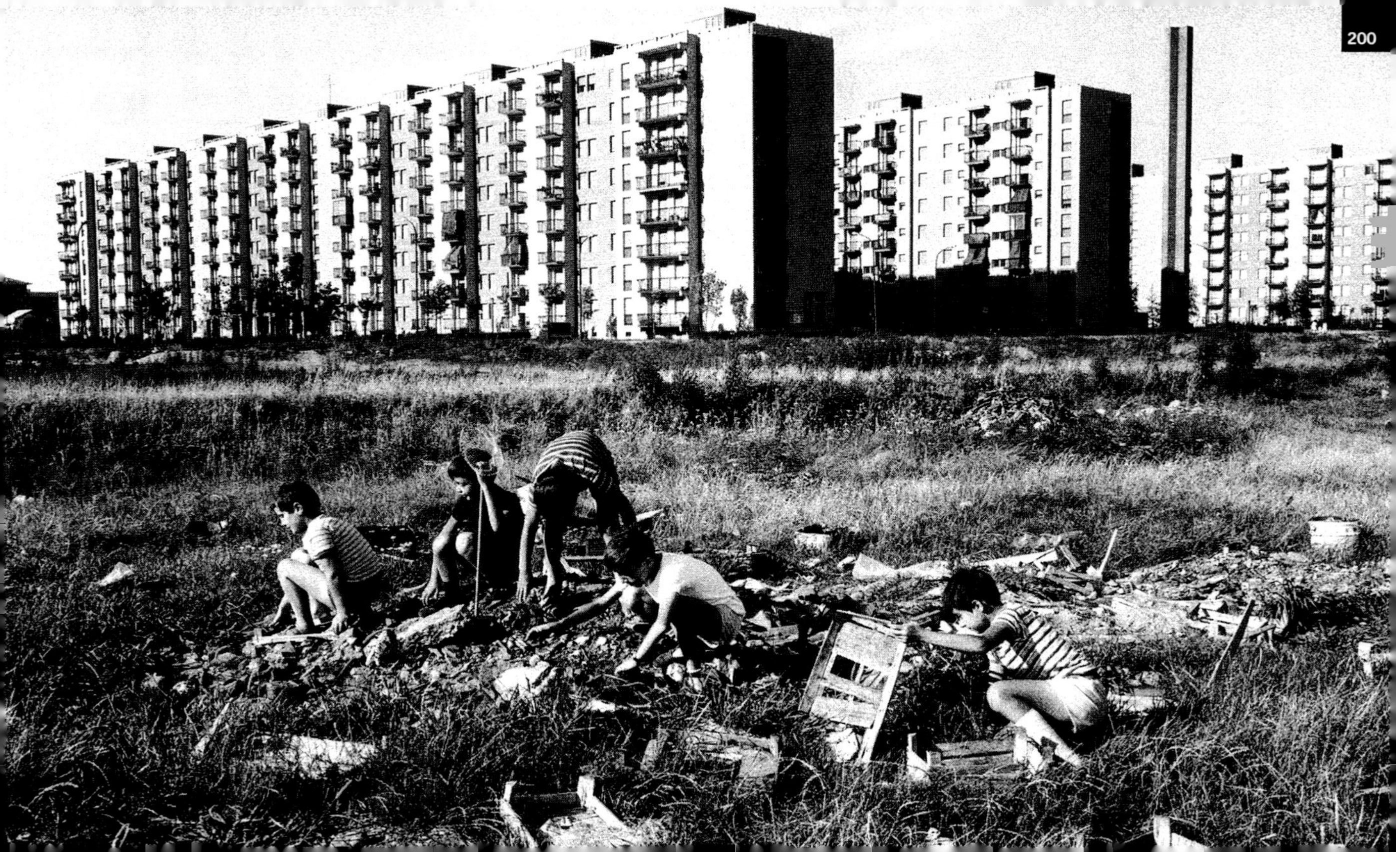

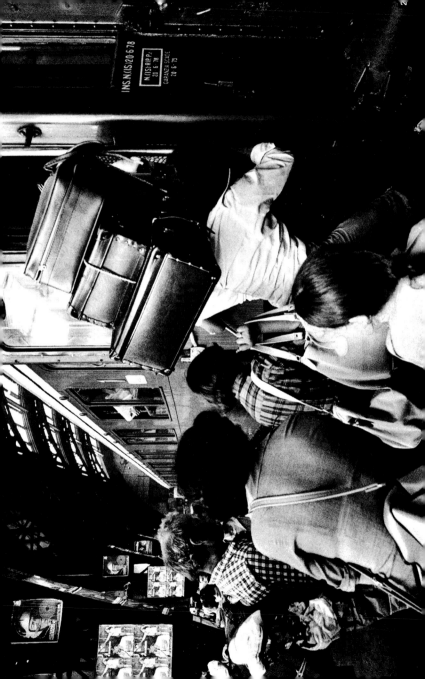

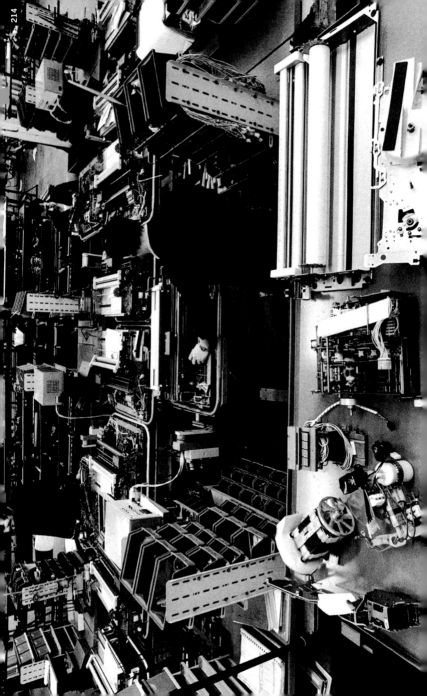

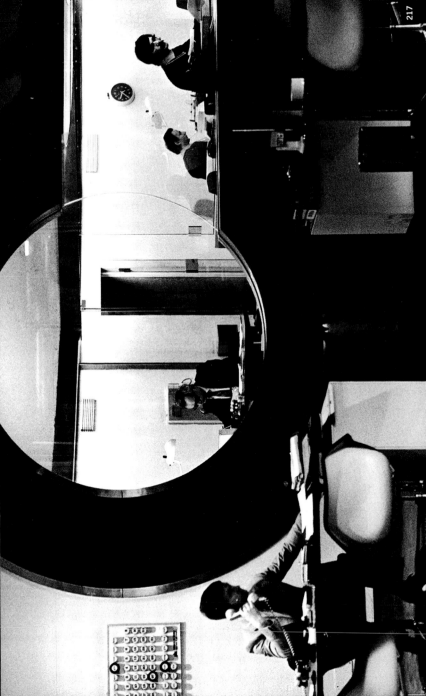

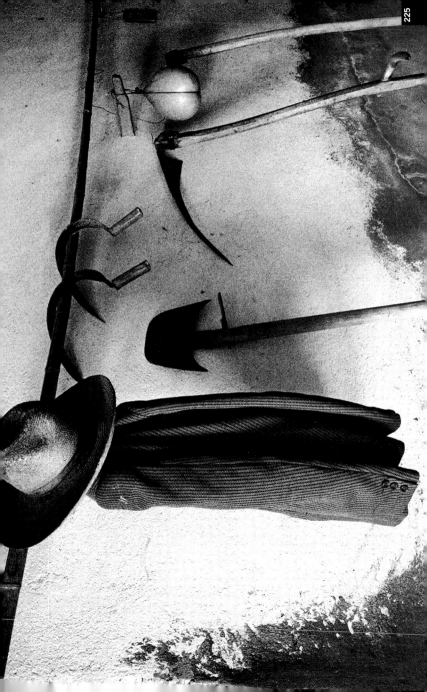

**1980-1989**

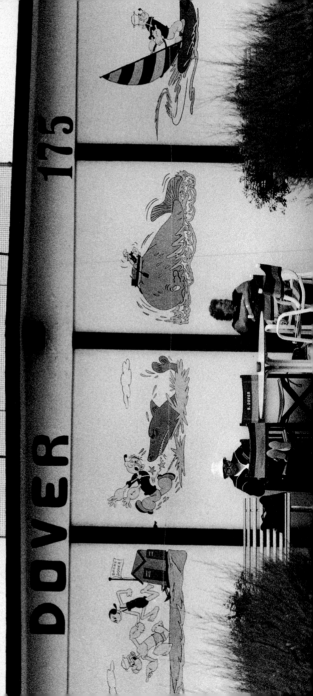

occhi sani
con collirio

STILLA

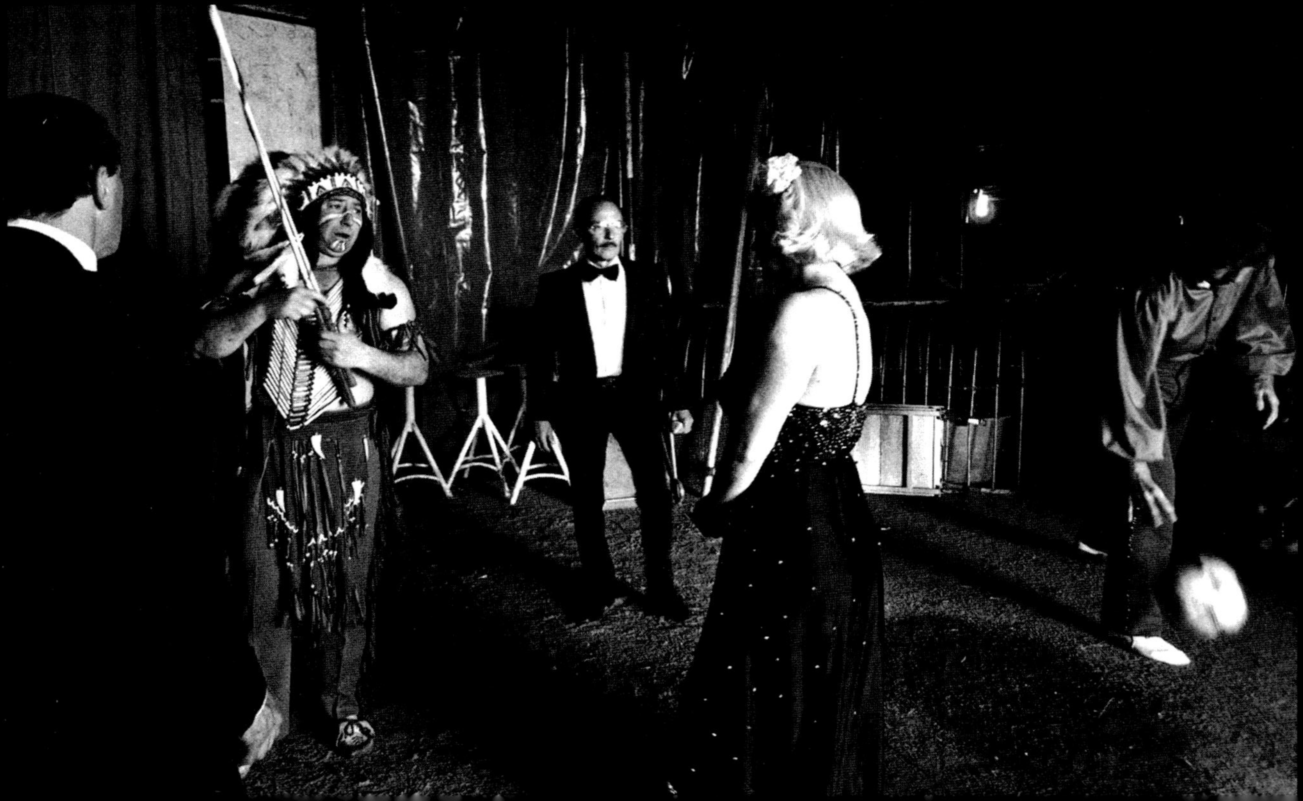

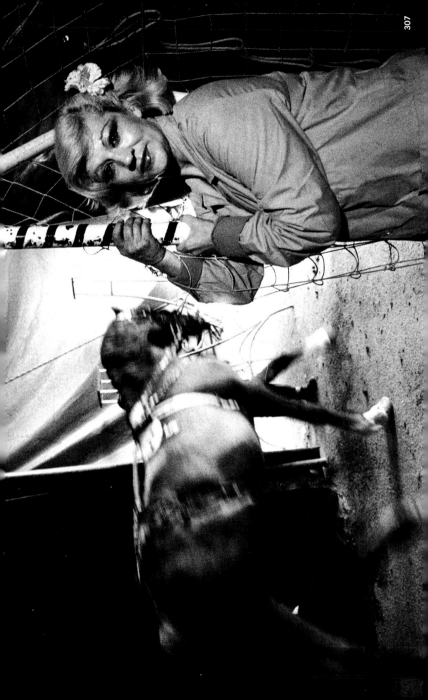

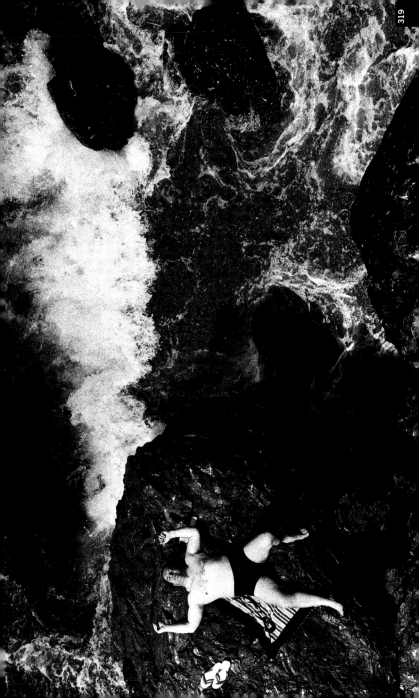

RIMOZIONE FORZATA
PER CONSENTIRE IL
TRANSITO DEI MEZZI
DI SOCCORSO
E DI SERVIZIO

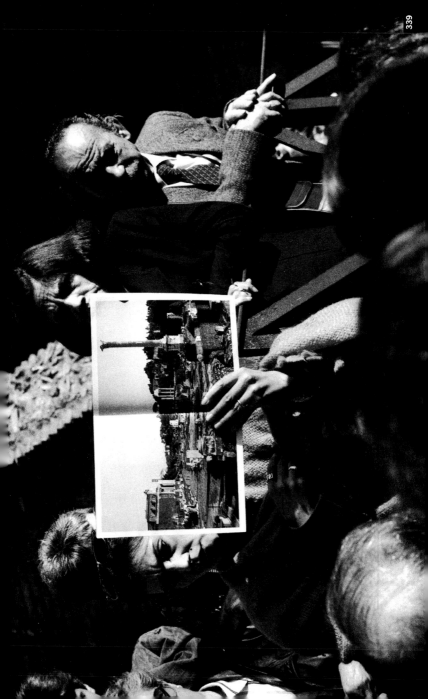

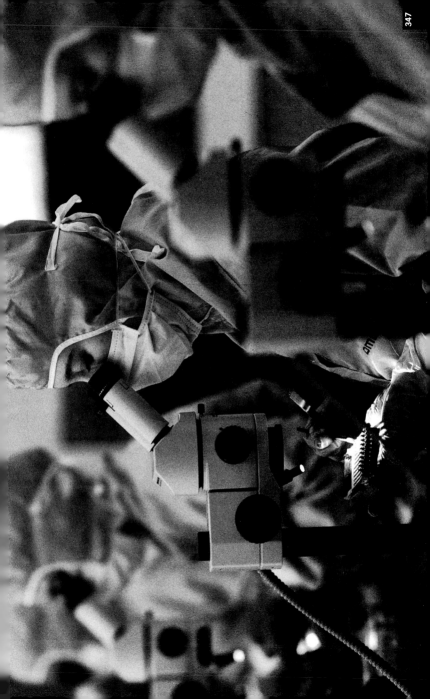

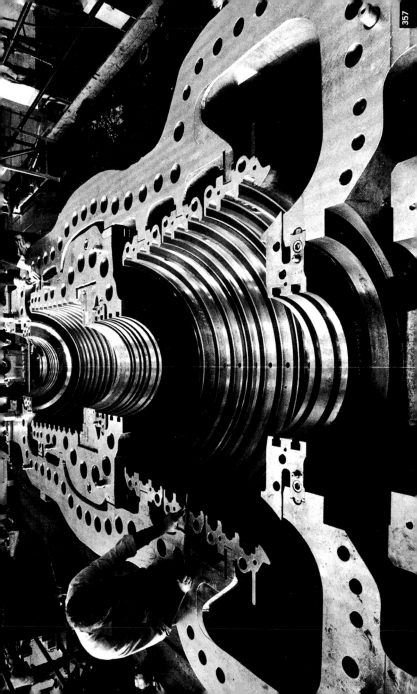

**1990-1999**

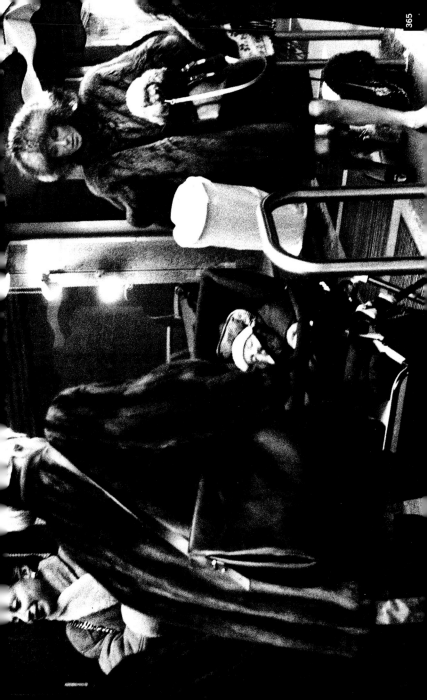

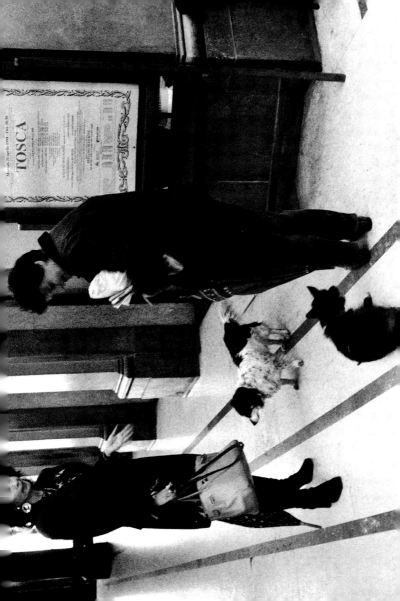

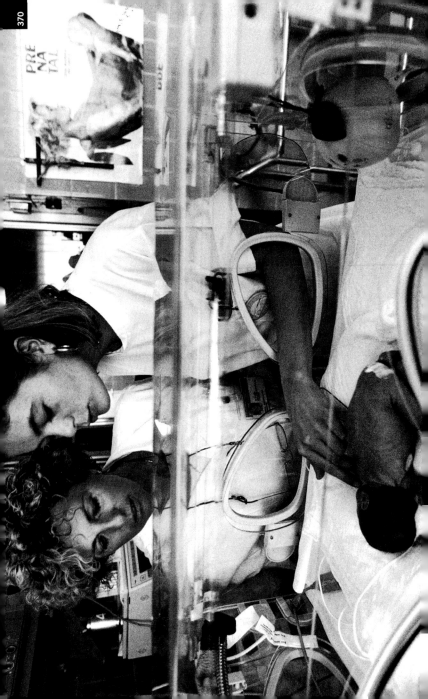

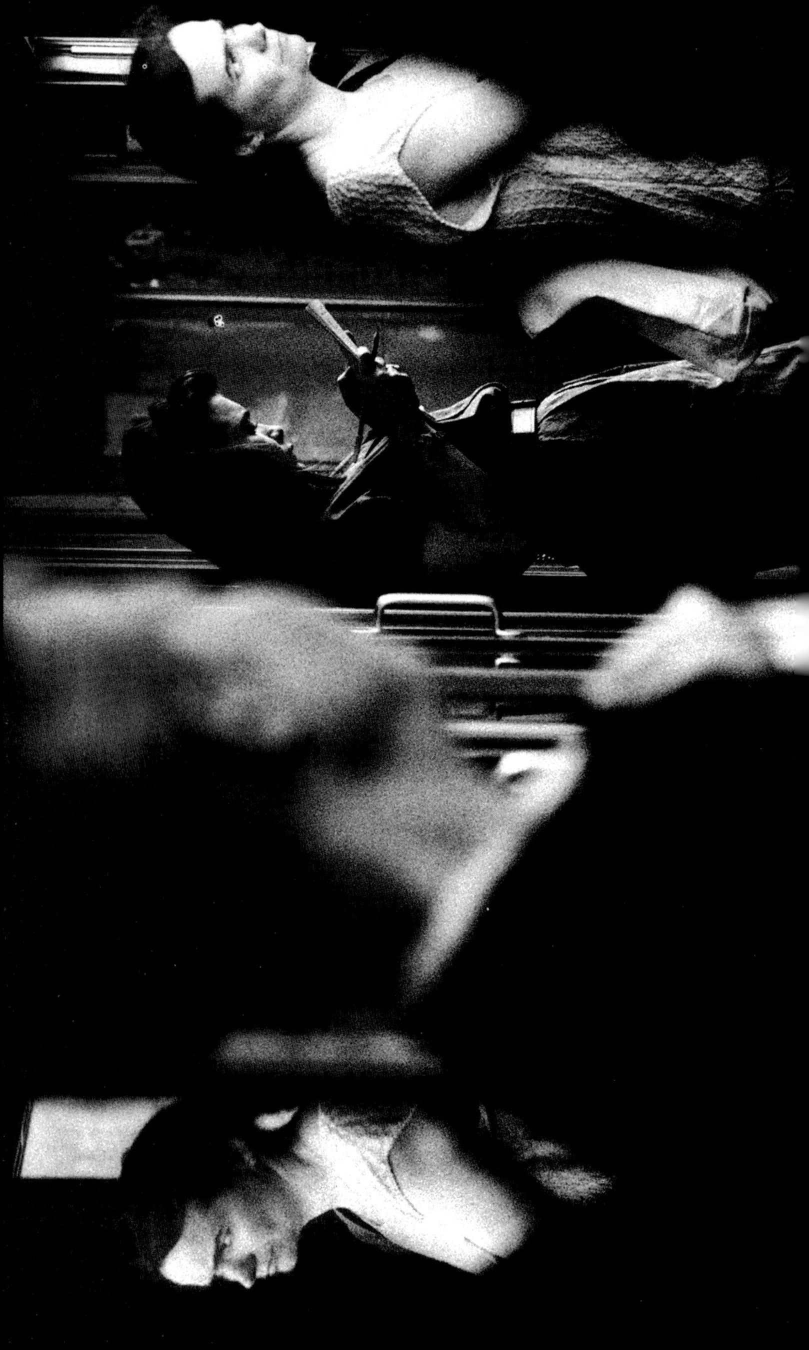

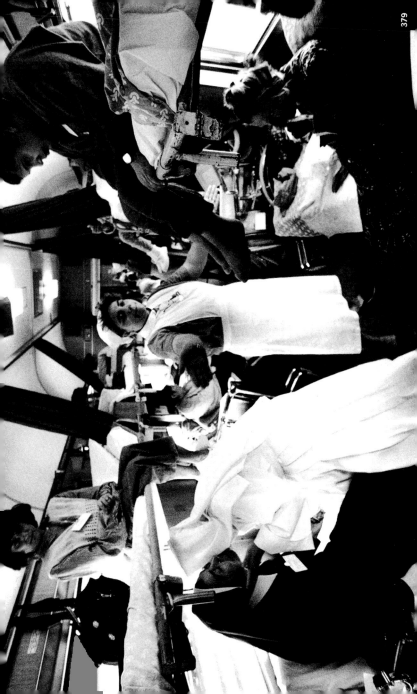

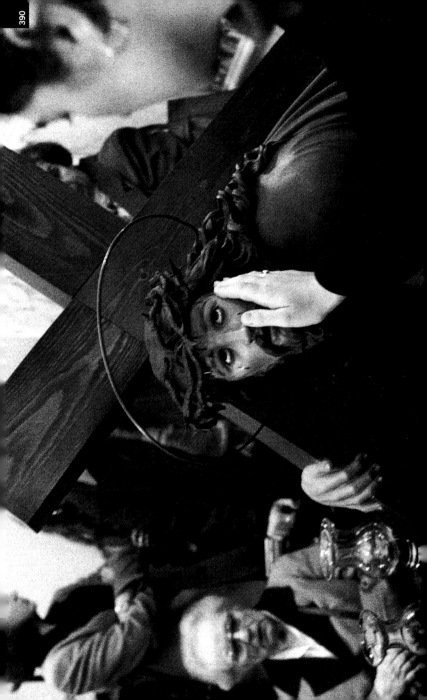

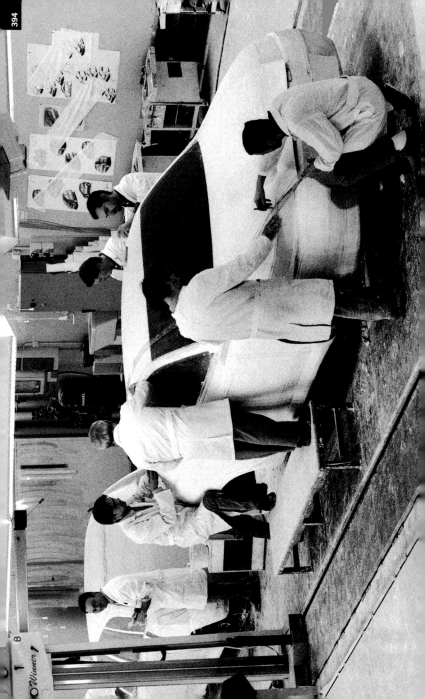

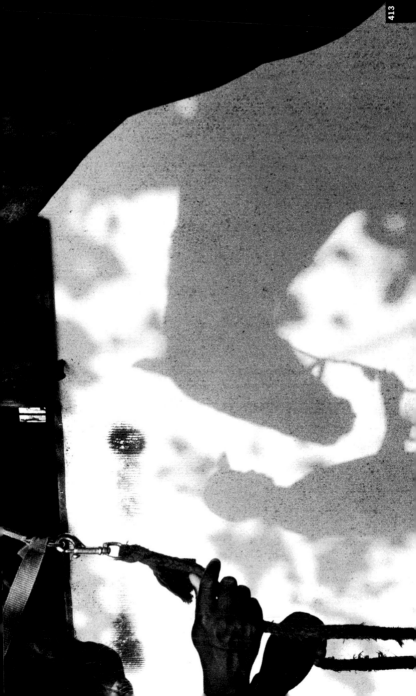

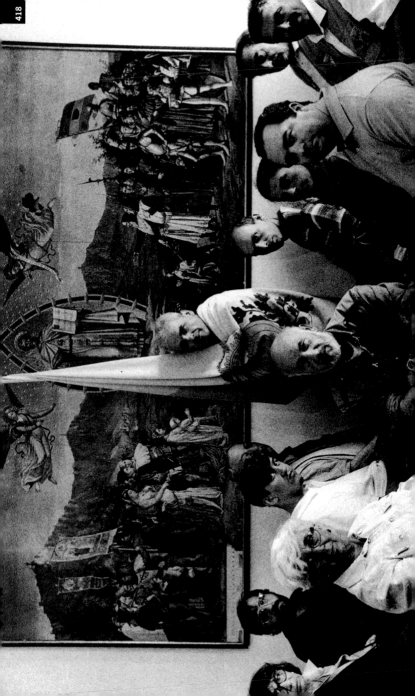

# VILLATA (VC)

FONDATA NEL 1884

SAGRA
DELLO
STRUZZO
dal 4 al 13
SETTEMBRE
198
TAVELLA
DI FIUME VENETO
SAGRA
STRUZZO

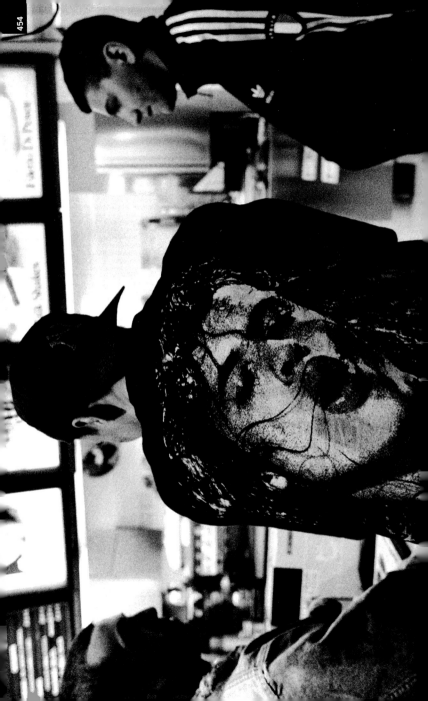

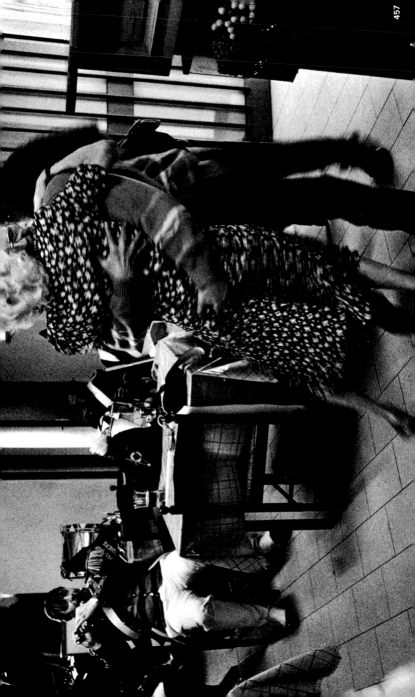

*La stagione di adesso,*

Printed and bound
by Arti Grafiche Motta
Milan, Italy